HOUGHTON MIFFLIN HARCOURT

JOURNEYS

Program Authors

James F. Baumann · David J. Chard · Jamal Cooks
J. David Cooper · Russell Gersten · Marjorie Lipson
Lesley Mandel Morrow · John J. Pikulski · Héctor H. Rivera
Mabel Rivera · Shane Templeton · Sheila W. Valencia
Catherine Valentino · MaryEllen Vogt

Consulting Author
Irene Fountas

HOUGHTON MIFFLIN HARCOURT
School Publishers

Hello, Reader!

What happens to living things as they grow? That's what the stories in this book are about. You will meet animals and children who are learning new things. You will even meet a silly pig who wonders if a piece of cheese and a dog bone will help his tree grow.

As you read, the number of words you know grows, too! Read on!

Sincerely,

The Authors

Watch Us Grow

Big Idea Living things change as they grow.

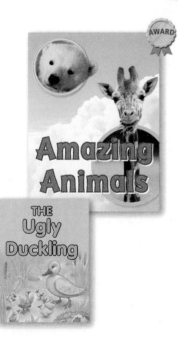

Lesson
24

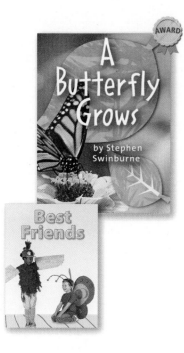

Watch Us Grow

Unit 5

Big Idea

Living things change as they grow.

Paired Selections

✔ **WORDS TO KNOW**
HIGH-FREQUENCY WORDS

told

night

pretty

window

thought

better

turned

saw

Vocabulary
Reader

Context
Cards

Words to Know

Read Together

- Read each Context Card.

- Choose two blue words.
  Use them in sentences.

1 told

He told the class the
name of the tree.

2 night

The buds open in the
day and close at night.

3 pretty

This is a **pretty** wide tree trunk!

4 window

The big tree is very close to the **window**.

5 thought

The man **thought** about planting a tree.

6 better

The tree got **better** when he watered it.

7 turned

The leaves **turned** orange in the fall.

8 saw

They **saw** many apples on the trees.

11

Background

✓ WORDS TO KNOW Life in a Tree

There is a tree outside my window. One day, I saw birds and squirrels in the tree. That night I thought I would take another look. I turned on a flashlight to see better. I saw an owl in the tree. I told my dad, "That tree is a pretty busy place!"

leaves

branch

trunk

bark

Find the parts of a tree in the picture. What other parts do you know?

Comprehension

Read Together

✓ **TARGET SKILL** Story Structure

Remember that a story has different parts. **Characters** are the people and animals in a story. The **setting** is when and where a story takes place. The **plot** is the order of story events. The events are often about a problem and how the characters solve it.

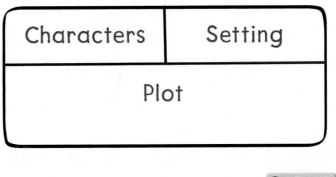

What is the problem?
How can it be solved?

After reading **The Tree**, tell who is in it, where they are, and what they do.

Characters	Setting
Plot	

JOURNEYS DIGITAL **Powered by** DESTINATIONReading®
Comprehension Activities: Lesson 21

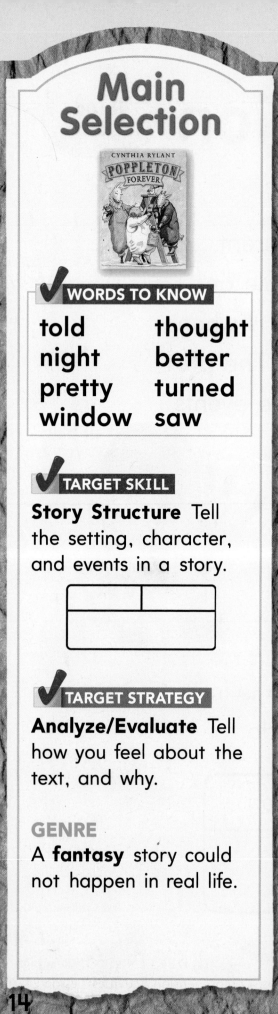
Meet the Author

Cynthia Rylant

As a young girl, Cynthia Rylant loved animals. She still does. Ms. Rylant lives with a dog and two cats. She puts animals in the books she writes, too.

Meet the Illustrator

Mark Teague

Mark Teague didn't go to art school. He taught himself to draw! He stays busy by working on more than one book at a time.

14

THE TREE

from POPPLETON FOREVER

by CYNTHIA RYLANT

illustrated by MARK TEAGUE

Essential Question

What do characters do when there is a problem?

Poppleton planted a new little tree
in his yard.
It was a dogwood.
Poppleton liked it very much.

He watered it every day.

He gave it tree food.

He staked it against the wind.

The little tree grew strong and fast.

Poppleton was pleased.

Then one day the tree looked awful.
Its leaves drooped.
Its bark peeled.
It turned from green to brown.
"Oh no!" said Poppleton,
when he saw his tree.

He called the tree doctor.
"Come right away!" said Poppleton.
The tree doctor came to look at
Poppleton's tree.

✔ STOP AND THINK
Story Structure How do you think Poppleton will solve his problem? Read to find out.

19

He tapped it. He stroked it.
He felt its trunk and leaves.
The tree doctor said to Poppleton,
"This tree needs something,
but I don't know what it is."

"Can't you just give it a pill?"
asked Poppleton.
"It isn't sick," said the tree doctor.
"It *needs* something."
Poppleton did not know
what his little tree needed.

He tapped it. He stroked it.
He felt its trunk and leaves.
But he did not know.
Poppleton sat up with his tree all
night, wondering what it needed.

In the morning he went for help.
"What does my tree need?" Poppleton
asked Hudson down the street.
"A piece of cheese?" said Hudson.
Poppleton gave the tree a piece
of cheese, but it didn't help.

"What does my tree need?" Poppleton
asked Newhouse, the delivery dog.
"A bone?" said Newhouse.

Poppleton gave the tree a
bone, but it didn't help.

Poppleton went to see Cherry Sue.
"What does my tree need?" Poppleton
asked Cherry Sue. Cherry Sue looked
out her window at the little tree.
She thought and thought.
Then she said, "If I were that tree,
I would need a bird feeder."

"A bird feeder?" asked Poppleton.
"Trees want birds," said Cherry
Sue. "Why do you think they hold
out their arms all day?"

Poppleton bought a bird feeder
for his little tree.

A sparrow came, and
a leaf turned green.

A cardinal came, and
another leaf turned green.

A bluebird came, and
three leaves turned green.

Poppleton's tree got better.

Soon all of its leaves were green.

"You are a pretty smart llama,"
Poppleton told Cherry Sue.

"You are a pretty nice pig," Cherry
Sue told him.

Then they had lemonade and watched
the birds.

Plant Care Tips

Write a Note What if Poppleton asked you how to take care of a new plant? Write him a note. Tell Poppleton some things he can do to make sure his plant does not get sick.
SCIENCE

Turn and Talk ## Problem Solved

Work with a partner. Talk about how each character in the story tries to help Poppleton solve his problem. Which character helps him the most? STORY STRUCTURE

31

Connect to Social Studies

GENRE

Informational text gives facts about a topic. Find facts about trees in this magazine article.

TEXT FOCUS

A **bar graph** is a drawing that uses bars to compare numbers. Use the graph on p. 34 to find facts about trees.

It Comes from Trees

by Russ Andrew

You may never have thought about all the things that are made from trees! Trees can be turned into many useful things. They help make our lives better day and night.

People use pretty much the whole tree to make things. Trees are cut into wood. The wood is used to build houses. Floors, doors, and window frames are made from wood.

Maybe you read a book or saw a poster today. The paper for those things is made from trees.

If someone told you that toothpaste and gum are made from trees, would you believe it? It's true!

This is one cord of wood. Look at the graph to see some paper products made from one cord of wood.

From One Cord of Wood

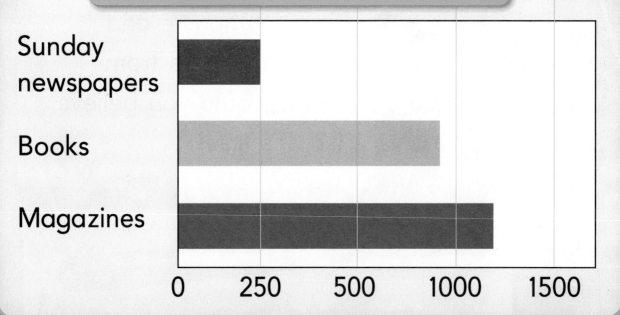

Making Connections

Text to Self

Connect to Experiences Think about how Poppleton cared for his tree. Write about something you have cared for.

Text to Text

List Ideas Why are the trees in both stories important? List your ideas.

Text to World

Think and Share Tell a partner how people help trees grow. Take turns listening. Speak clearly.

Grammar

Subject Pronouns Words that can take the place of nouns are called **pronouns**. The pronouns **he**, **she**, and **it** name one. The pronouns **we** and **they** name more than one.

Ben watered the tree. **He** watered the tree.
The tree grew. **It** grew.
Birds loved the tree. **They** loved the tree.
Lily fed the birds. **She** fed the birds.

Choose the correct pronoun to name each picture. Write it on a sheet of paper. Then say a sentence to a partner about each picture. Use the pronoun.

1.		she	he
2.		they	it
3.		it	we
4.		they	she
5.		we	he

Grammar in Writing

When you proofread your writing, be sure you have used pronouns correctly.

Write to Express

Ideas Story **sentences** can tell the exact words characters say. These words help us understand how characters think and feel.

Niki wrote what Poppleton did next. Then she added words that told just what he said.

Revised Draft

Now Poppleton was hungry.
"I want some pizza," he said.
^Cherry Sue was hungry, too.

Writing Traits Checklist

Ideas Did I write the exact words a character says?

✓ Do I need to add interesting details?

✓ Did I use pronouns correctly?

38

Look for the exact words Poppleton said in Niki's final copy. Then revise your own writing. Use the Checklist.

Snack Time

Now Poppleton was hungry.

"I want some pizza," he said.

Cherry Sue was hungry, too.

So they hopped on bikes

and went to a pizza shop.

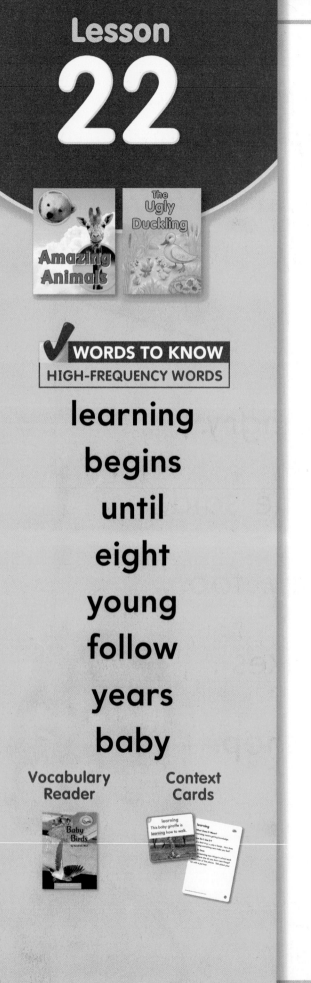

✔ **WORDS TO KNOW**
HIGH-FREQUENCY WORDS

learning

begins

until

eight

young

follow

years

baby

Vocabulary
Reader

Context
Cards

Words to Know

● Read each Context Card.

● Make up a new sentence that uses a blue word.

1 **learning**
This baby giraffe is learning how to walk.

2 **begins**
The lion cub begins to get stronger.

3 until

These owls can't fly until they are older.

4 eight

The eight little swans go for a swim.

5 young

The young hippo will be very big soon.

6 follow

The bear cubs follow their mother.

7 years

An elephant can live for seventy years.

8 baby

This baby panda is eating plants.

Background

Read Together

✔ **WORDS TO KNOW** **Growing Up**

Many baby animals need help until they grow older. Young animals are learning as they follow their mothers around. A baby elephant may stay with its mother for many years. A kitten begins to care for itself before it is eight weeks old.

Animals and Their Babies

cat

kitten

bear   cub

elephant   calf   duck   duckling

Comprehension

✔ TARGET SKILL Conclusions

When you draw **conclusions**, you use details as clues to figure out things the author doesn't tell. Good readers find clues in the words and in the pictures. They also think about what they know from their own life.

Conclusion: The children are going to school. What clues helped you?

As you read **Amazing Animals**, draw conclusions about why different animals have different body parts.

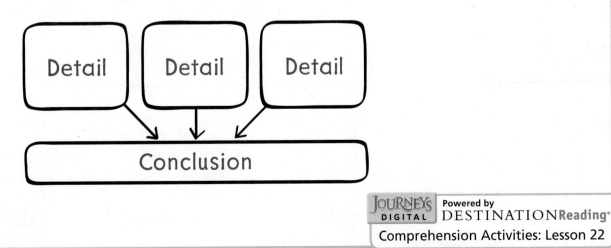

| Detail | Detail | Detail |

Conclusion

JOURNEYS DIGITAL Powered by DESTINATIONReading®
Comprehension Activities: Lesson 22

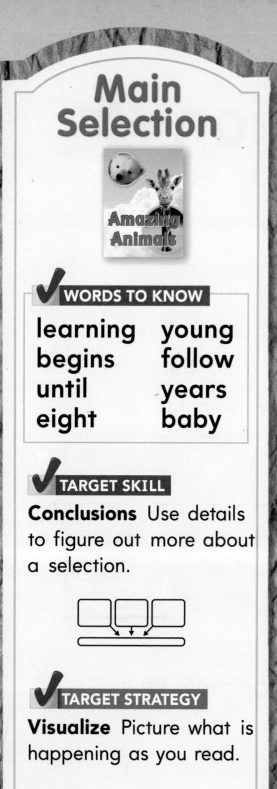

Amazing Animals

✔ **WORDS TO KNOW**

learning	young
begins	follow
until	years
eight	baby

✔ **TARGET SKILL**

Conclusions Use details to figure out more about a selection.

✔ **TARGET STRATEGY**

Visualize Picture what is happening as you read.

GENRE
Informational text gives facts about a topic.

Meet the Author

Gwendolyn Hooks

Gwendolyn Hooks wrote this story because she loves animals. "This story is about wild animals," she explains.

"I don't own any wild animals, but I do have a pet cat."

Amazing Animals

by
Gwendolyn
Hooks

Essential Question

What clues tell you
why animals look
as they do?

Big eyes,

long beak,

thick fur,

big squeak!

Animals get a lot of help as they grow up. Let's find out about eight amazing animals.

Polar Bear

A polar bear has thick fur. Each hair is like a tube. The hair has no color, like glass. The sun makes it look white.

How does thick, white fur help?

Thick fur helps polar bears stay warm. The color of their fur looks the same as snow. This helps them hide.

Where does this cute young polar bear like to hide?

Elephant

An elephant has a long nose. The nose is called a trunk. It takes many years for an elephant to grow two big teeth. These teeth are called tusks.

How do tusks and a trunk help?

Elephants use their tusks to scrape bark off trees. Then they eat the bark. These elephants are learning to use their trunks to get water.

Sometimes they will spray water at a friend!

Camel

Some camels have one hump.
Some have two. All camels
have two rows of eyelashes.

How do humps and thick
eyelashes help?

A camel's hump has fat inside. On long trips, a camel's body uses the fat for food. A camel's eyelashes keep out the desert sand.

This baby camel will follow his mother when the herd goes from place to place.

Duck

A duck is a bird. It has two feet, and each foot has three toes. A duck has a beak, too.

How do feet and a beak help?

Ducks use their feet to swim in the water or walk on land. They use their beaks to eat plants and bugs.

Look! This duck uses her beak to clean her friend.

Giraffe

A giraffe has spots. A giraffe has a long neck.

How do spots and a long neck help?

A giraffe's spots help it hide. A giraffe's long neck helps it reach the leaves of trees.

This giraffe's long neck helps her reach her baby. She gives him a big kiss!

Porcupine

A porcupine has soft quills when it is born. The quills get sharp in a day or two.

How do quills help?

Quills help keep a porcupine safe. If an animal begins to come too close, the porcupine backs into it. The sharp quills hurt!

Quills tell this cub to stay away!

✔ STOP AND THINK
Conclusions
Why would a porcupine want animals to stay away?

Turtle

A turtle has a shell that is very hard.

How does a hard shell help?

A turtle can hide inside its shell
from an animal that may hurt it.
The turtle waits until the animal
goes away. Then the turtle comes
back out.

You're safe now, turtle!

Dolphin

A dolphin's tail has two parts called flukes. A dolphin has two flippers.

How do tail flukes and flippers help?

A dolphin flips its tail flukes up and down to swim fast. It uses its flippers to turn to the left or right.

These two dolphins swim away fast. Who will be first?

Have fun, dolphins!

Your Turn

Animal Body Parts

Draw and Label Which animal in **Amazing Animals** do you think is the most amazing? Draw a picture of it and label its body parts. Tell how special body parts help that animal. SCIENCE

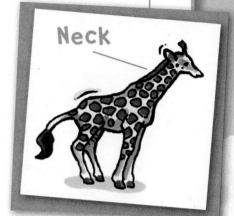

Neck

Turn and Talk — Hiding Animals

Look back through the selection with a partner. Which animals have body parts that help them hide? Talk about why animals might need to hide. CONCLUSIONS

Connect to Traditional Tales

✔ **WORDS TO KNOW**

learning	young
begins	follow
until	years
eight	baby

GENRE

A **fairy tale** is an old story with characters that can do amazing things.

TEXT FOCUS

Many fairy tales begin **Once upon a time** and end **happily ever after.** What do these words mean in this story?

The Ugly Duckling

Once upon a time, a duck sat on eight eggs. One day, all but one of the eggs hatched. The ducks waited until the last baby bird came out. He was big and gray. The other ducks thought he was ugly.

Each day the ducklings would follow
Mother Duck. They were learning to be
ducks. The other ducks did not want to
play with the ugly duckling. He felt sad.
One day he left.

Winter soon came. A farmer found the
ugly duckling. "I must take you home
before it begins to snow," he said.

When spring came, the farmer took the duckling to a pond. The duckling saw himself in the water. He felt like many years had passed. He had changed!

Now he knew he was not an ugly duckling. He was a young swan. He and the other swans lived happily ever after.

Making Connections

Read Together

Text to Self

Write Sentences Draw your favorite animal. Write sentences to tell your classmates about it.

Text to Text

Compare Selections Which selection is true? Which selection is make-believe? Talk about your answer with three classmates. Be sure to speak clearly.

Text to World

Connect to Science What is the same about how baby animals and baby children grow? What is different? Tell your ideas. Take turns with a partner.

Grammar

Read Together

The Pronoun I Always use the **pronoun I** in the subject of a sentence. Name yourself last when you talk about yourself and another person.

Correct

Sara and I like baby animals.

Not Correct

I and Sara like baby animals.
Sara and me like baby animals.
Me and Sara like baby animals.

Write the correct words to finish each
sentence. Use another sheet of paper.
Read your sentences to a partner.

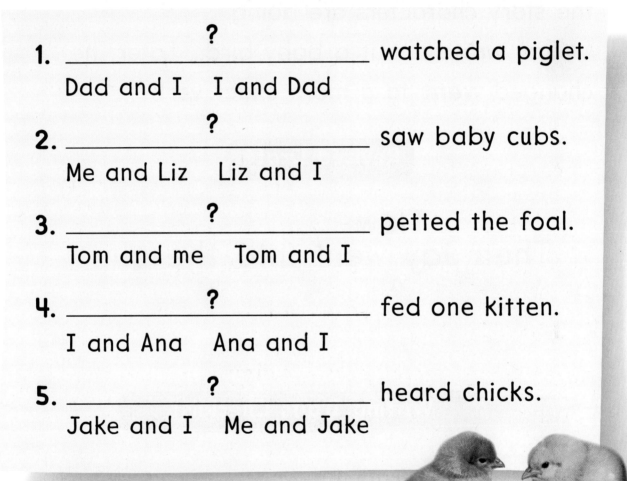

1. _____?_____ watched a piglet.
   Dad and I   I and Dad

2. _____?_____ saw baby cubs.
   Me and Liz   Liz and I

3. _____?_____ petted the foal.
   Tom and me   Tom and I

4. _____?_____ fed one kitten.
   I and Ana   Ana and I

5. _____?_____ heard chicks.
   Jake and I   Me and Jake

Grammar in Writing

When you proofread your writing, be sure
you have used the pronoun **I** correctly.
Remember to capitalize the prounoun **I**.

69

Write to Express

☑ **Word Choice** Good story **sentences** have exact verbs that help readers picture what the story characters are doing.

Troy wrote about a baby bird. Later, he changed **went** to a more exact verb.

Revised Draft

flew
Then Jay ~~went~~ into the air.
               ∧

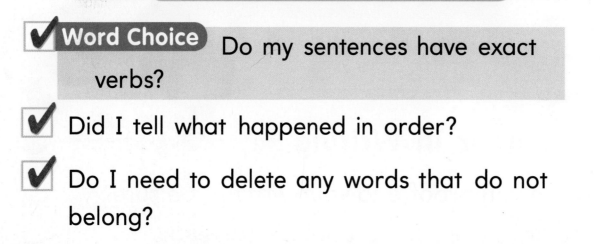

Writing Traits Checklist

☑ **Word Choice** Do my sentences have exact verbs?

☑ Did I tell what happened in order?

☑ Do I need to delete any words that do not belong?

Look for exact verbs in Troy's final copy.
Then revise your writing. Use the Checklist.

Final Copy

Flying Lesson

Jay stood quietly by the nest.

First, he watched his mom.

Then Jay flew into the air.

He sailed high above
the garden.

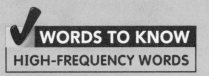
WORDS TO KNOW
HIGH-FREQUENCY WORDS

house

along

together

boy

father

again

nothing

began

Vocabulary
Reader

Context
Cards

Words to Know

- Read each Context Card.

- Ask a question that uses one of the blue words.

1
house
They learned how to build a house for birds.

2
along
He rode carefully along the bike path.

3 together

The baby can clap her hands together now.

4 boy

The boy teaches his sister to read.

5 father

My father teaches me how to swim.

6 again

We went out on the ice again to practice.

7 nothing

At first nothing fit, but he finished the puzzle.

8 began

She began to take violin lessons.

Background

✓ **WORDS TO KNOW** **Puppy Training**

A boy and his father were teaching their puppy to walk on a leash. They walked together along a path. Suddenly the leash dropped, and the puppy began to run. Nothing could stop her. The boy whistled again and again. At last, the puppy came to him. They all walked back to the house.

- What pets do you like?
- What would you teach a pet to do?

Comprehension

✔ **TARGET SKILL** **Cause and Effect**

Sometimes one story event causes another event to happen. The **cause** happens first. It is the reason why something else happens. The **effect** is what happens next. Good readers think about:

What happened?
Why did it happen?

Cause: The light turned red. What is the **effect**?

As you read **Whistle for Willie**, think about what happens when Peter tries to whistle.

What happens?	Why?

Main Selection

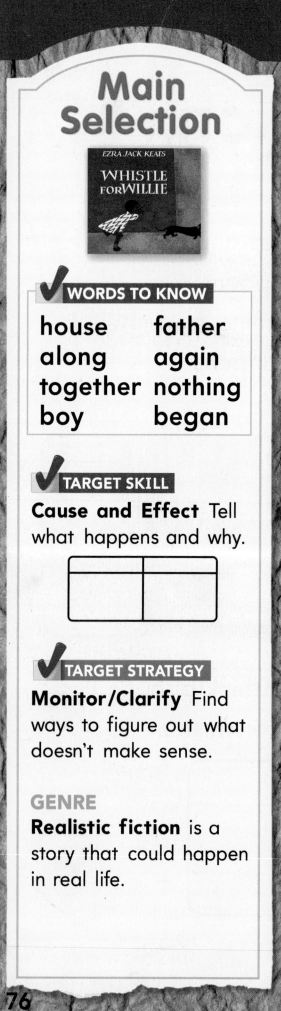

EZRA JACK KEATS
WHISTLE for WILLIE

✔ WORDS TO KNOW

house	father
along	again
together	nothing
boy	began

✔ TARGET SKILL

Cause and Effect Tell what happens and why.

✔ TARGET STRATEGY

Monitor/Clarify Find ways to figure out what doesn't make sense.

GENRE

Realistic fiction is a story that could happen in real life.

Meet the Author and Illustrator

Ezra Jack Keats

Ezra Jack Keats wrote and illustrated books for children. When Mr. Keats was a boy, he drew pictures on the kitchen table. His mother was so proud, she kept the art rather than wash the table.

WHISTLE FOR WILLIE

by Ezra Jack Keats

Oh, how Peter wished he could whistle!

He saw a boy playing with his dog. Whenever the boy whistled, the dog ran straight to him.

Peter tried and tried to whistle, but he couldn't. So instead he began to turn himself around—
around and around he whirled . . .
faster and faster . . . .
When he stopped
everything turned
down . . .
and up . . .

and up . . .
and down . . .
and around
and around.

Peter saw his dog, Willie, coming.
Quick as a wink, he hid in an empty
carton lying on the sidewalk.

"Wouldn't it be funny if I whistled?" Peter thought. "Willie would stop and look all around to see who it was."

Peter tried again to whistle—but still he couldn't. So Willie just walked on.

✔ **STOP AND THINK**
Cause and Effect What do you think will happen if Peter tries to whistle again? Read to find out.

Peter got out of the carton and started home.
On the way he took some colored chalks out
of his pocket and drew a long, long line
right up to his door.

He stood there and tried to whistle
again. He blew till his cheeks were
tired. But nothing happened.

He went into his house and put on his father's old hat to make himself feel more grown-up. He looked into the mirror to practice whistling. Still no whistle!

When his mother saw what he was doing,
Peter pretended that he was his father.
He said, "I've come home early today, dear.
Is Peter here?"
His mother answered, "Why no, he's outside
with Willie."
"Well, I'll go out and look for them," said Peter.

First he walked along a crack in the
sidewalk. Then he tried to run away
from his shadow.

He jumped off his shadow.
But when he landed
they were
together
again.

He came to the corner
where the carton was,
and who should he see
but Willie!

Peter scrambled under the carton.
He blew and blew.
Suddenly—out came a real whistle!

Willie stopped and looked around to
see who it was.

"It's me," Peter shouted, and stood up.
Willie raced straight to him.

Peter ran home to show his father and
mother what he could do.
They loved Peter's whistling. So did Willie.

Peter's mother asked him and Willie
to go on an errand to the grocery store.
He whistled all the way there,
and he whistled all the way home.

Willie's Words

Write Sentences

What would Willie say if he could talk? Write sentences that tell the story the way Willie would tell it. PERSONAL RESPONSE

Turn and Talk — What Happened?

Read pages 90–93 again with a partner. Tell what happens when Peter tries to whistle. How is it different from the first time Peter tried to whistle? CAUSE AND EFFECT

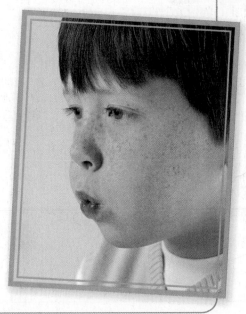

![Pet Poems]

Connect to Poetry

GENRE

Poetry uses words to show pictures and feelings. Listen for interesting words in each poem. Clap along with the rhythm, or beat.

TEXT FOCUS

Rhyme is words with the same ending sound. Which poems use rhyme?

Pet Poems

This poem began as a folk song. Read it along with your class. Then sing it together.

Bingo

There was a farmer had a dog,
And Bingo was his name, O!
B – I – N – G – O,
B – I – N – G – O,
B – I – N – G – O,

And Bingo was his name, O!

Can someone in your class read this poem
in Spanish? Now read it again in English.

Caballito blanco, reblanco

Caballito blanco,
reblanco,
sácame de aquí,
llévame hasta el puerto
donde yo nací.

Little White Horse

Little horse
White as snow
Take me where
I long to go.
Take me to the port
By the sea
Where I was born
And long to be.

traditional folk poem

99

What kind of pet would you like in your house? Your mother or father can help you decide.

PET SNAKE

No trace of fuzz.
No bit of fur.
No growling bark,
or gentle purr.
No cozy cuddle.
No sloppy kiss.
All he really does
is hisssssssssss.

by Rebecca Kai Dotlich

Write About a Pet

Write a poem about a pet. Use words with the same beginning sounds. Try to use the words boy and nothing, too.

Making Connections

Read Together

Text to Self

Talk About Pets Tell a partner about a pet you would like to have. Take turns and speak clearly.

Text to Text

Make a Poster How is Willie different from the pet snake in the poem? Draw Willie. Write words that tell what he looks like and what he can do.

Text to World

Connect to Math Make a list of pets. Count how many classmates like each kind of pet.

Grammar

Read Together

Possessive Pronouns Some **pronouns** show that something belongs to someone. This kind of pronoun can come before a noun or at the end of a sentence.

This is **my** dog.
This dog is **mine**.

I am using **your** chalk.
The chalk is **yours**.

That is **his** shadow.
That shadow is **his**.

I am wearing **her** hat.
This hat is **hers**.

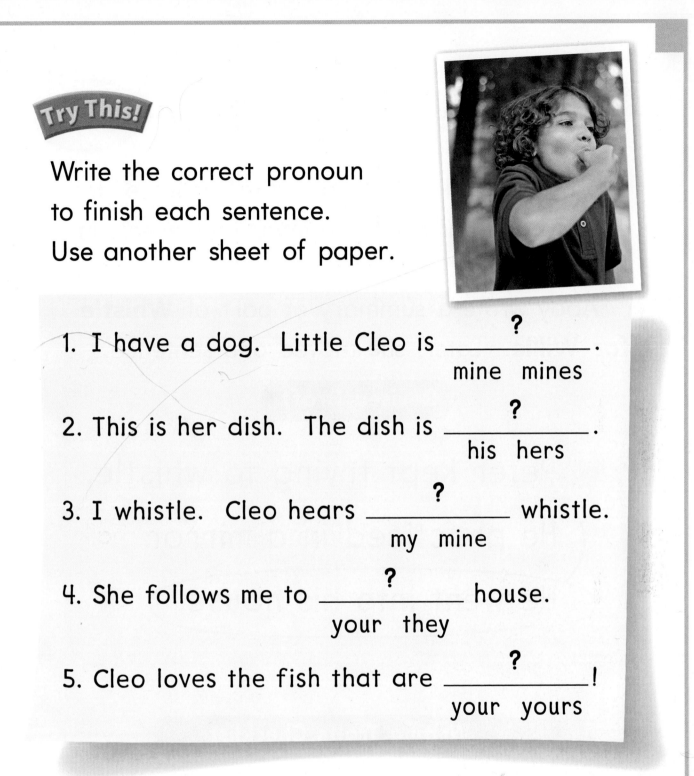

Write the correct pronoun
to finish each sentence.
Use another sheet of paper.

1. I have a dog. Little Cleo is _____**?**___.
   mine   mines

2. This is her dish. The dish is _____**?**___.
   his   hers

3. I whistle. Cleo hears _____**?**__ whistle.
   my   mine

4. She follows me to _____**?**__ house.
   your   they

5. Cleo loves the fish that are _____**?**__!
   your   yours

Grammar in Writing

When you proofread your writing, be sure
you have used pronouns correctly.

Write to Express

Read Together

✓ **Organization** When you write sentences for a story **summary**, tell the important events in the order they happened.

Abby wrote a summary of part of **Whistle for Willie**. Later, she moved one sentence.

Revised Draft

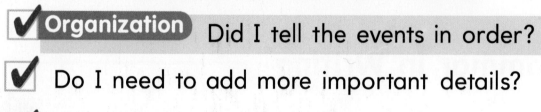

Peter kept trying to whistle.

He practiced in a mirror.

He went into his house.

Writing Traits Checklist

✓ **Organization** Did I tell the events in order?

✓ Do I need to add more important details?

✓ Did I use the correct pronouns?

Look for events in the correct order in Abby's final copy. Then revise your own writing. Use the Checklist.

Final Copy

Whistle for Willie

Peter kept trying to whistle.

Then he went into his house.

He practiced in a mirror.

When his mom saw him, he pretended to be his dad.

Lesson 24

✓ WORDS TO KNOW
HIGH-FREQUENCY WORDS

ready

anything

upon

kind

places

also

flower

warm

Vocabulary Reader

Context Cards

Words to Know

Read Together

- Read each Context Card.
- Describe a picture, using the blue word.

1

ready

This butterfly is getting ready to fly.

2

anything

Do you know anything about butterflies?

106

3 upon

A butterfly rests upon the leaf.

4 kind

There is more than one kind of butterfly.

5 places

Butterflies land on this tree in many places.

6 also

Butterflies are insects. Ants are also insects.

7 flower

This butterfly drinks from the flower.

8 warm

Butterflies like the warm sun.

Background

✔ WORDS TO KNOW **A Caterpillar's Story**

I grew in an egg, and now I crawl. I do not eat anything but a special kind of leaf. I'm eating a lot and also growing quickly. When I am ready, I will change. Then I'll be able to fly to warm places. I'll find a pretty flower to sit upon. What do you learn about me from my picture?

Monarch Caterpillar

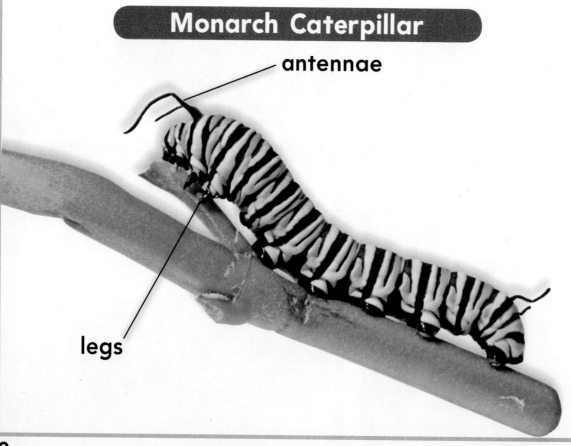

antennae

legs

Comprehension

Read Together

✓ TARGET SKILL Sequence of Events

Many selections tell about things in the order in which they happen. This order is called the **sequence of events**. Think about what happens first, next, and last as you read.

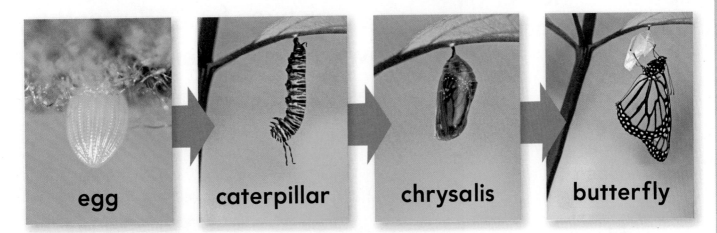

egg   caterpillar   chrysalis   butterfly

As you read **A Butterfly Grows**, think about how a caterpillar becomes a butterfly. Use a chart to keep track of the sequence of events.

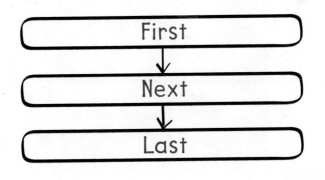

First

Next

Last

Main Selection

A Butterfly Grows by Stephen Swinburne

✔ WORDS TO KNOW

ready	places
anything	also
upon	flower
kind	warm

✔ TARGET SKILL

Sequence of Events
Tell the order in which things happen.

✔ TARGET STRATEGY

Question Ask questions about what you read.

GENRE

Narrative nonfiction gives facts but has make-believe parts.

Meet the Author

Steve Swinburne

Steve Swinburne loves nature—especially butterflies! He planted a garden at his house filled with flowers that butterflies like. He took many of the pictures for **A Butterfly Grows** in his garden. He hopes you enjoy learning about butterflies.

A Butterfly Grows

by Stephen Swinburne

Essential Question

Why do authors put events in a certain order?

Can you see me
on the plant?

I am a little caterpillar!
I grew in an egg. When I
was ready, I hatched!

The wind blows. I hang onto
a branch so I don't fall.

Rain falls. It plips and plops.
I need to drink water to live,
so I drink the small drops.

This milkweed plant is my food.
I need food so I can grow.

I eat this leaf for lunch.
Chew, chew!
Crunch, munch!

I eat and grow,
eat and grow.

Look how big I grew!
My skin is so snug.

I look for a spot to rest.
Soon I will shed my skin.

At last I am a chrysalis. I'm
an inch long. Then, in ten days,
I am ready to come out.

✓ **STOP AND THINK**
Sequence of Events
What will the caterpillar look like after
it comes out? Read on to find out.

Look at me now!
Do you see anything new?

I am an insect now.
I have six legs and
large wings.

My wings help me fly. Watch me fly!
I have fun! My wings also help me
go find plants for food.

I like to fly with all my friends.
We fly to warm places in the fall.
We eat food along the way.

I land upon a flower. Watch me
eat now! I sip and sip. Do you
know what kind of insect I am?

I am a butterfly!
I'm a beautiful butterfly!

A Butterfly's Life

Draw and Order Divide a sheet of paper into three boxes. Draw a stage of the butterfly's life in each box and label it. Cut out the pictures and mix them up. Give them to a partner. Have your partner put them in order. PARTNERS

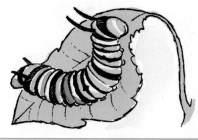

Turn and Talk — Order of Events

Talk with a partner about the order of events in **A Butterfly Grows**. Do you think the author could have put any of the events in a different order? Tell why or why not. SEQUENCE OF EVENTS

Connect to Science

GENRE

Readers' theater is text that has been written for people to read aloud.

TEXT FOCUS

Dialogue is the speaking parts in a play. You learn about characters from what they say. After reading, describe the characters.

Readers' Theater

Best Friends

by Stephen Gill

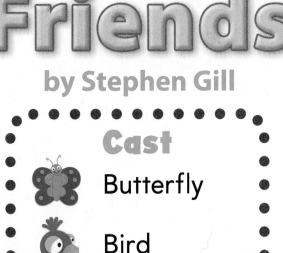

Cast

Butterfly

Bird

 Hi! What kind of butterfly are you?

 I'm not a butterfly, silly. Can you think of anything else I could be?

 Give me some clues!

 Okay. I grow in an egg, and then I hatch.

Me, too!

 I have wings to help me fly.

 Me, too!

 I eat seeds and insects.

 Oh, no! I am an insect. Will you eat me?

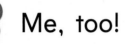 No! Birds like me eat many insects, but not butterflies.

You just said you are a bird!

Oops, silly me! You know what I am!

 Are you ready to find a snack? I'll land upon a flower and sip and sip. You can find an insect on a leaf.

 We can also fly together. Then we'll find warm places to rest.

 What a nice day for two best friends!

Making Connections

Text to Self

Write a Response Write about a day you spend with the butterfly in **A Butterfly Grows**. Tell what you do.

Text to Text

Connect to Science What facts did you learn from the selections? Which parts of these selections are make-believe? How do you know?

Text to World

Describe a Friend Draw a picture of you and your best friend having fun together. Tell a partner reasons why your best friend is your favorite.

Grammar

Read Together

Pronouns and Verbs Add **s** to most **verbs** when they tell about a **pronoun** that names one.

One	More Than One
It eat**s**.	They eat.
He grow**s**.	We grow.

Use **am** with the pronoun **I**. Use **is** with other pronouns that name one. Use **are** with pronouns that name more than one.

One	More Than One
I **am** hungry.	We **are** hungry.
She **is** full.	They **are** full.

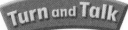

Write the correct verb to finish each sentence. Use another sheet of paper. Take turns reading the sentences with a partner.

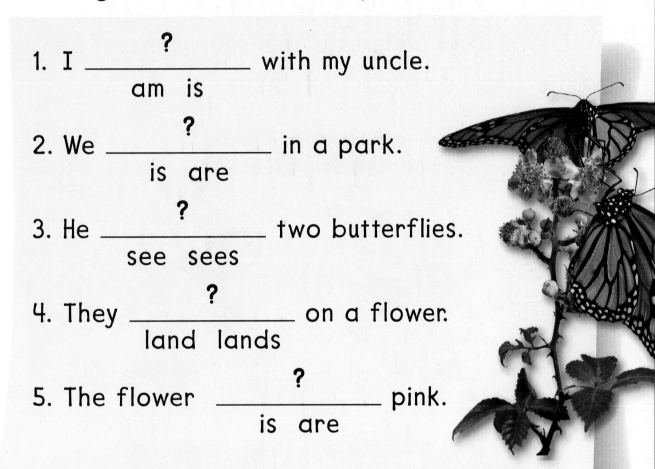

1. I _____ with my uncle.
   am is

2. We _____ in a park.
   is are

3. He _____ two butterflies.
   see sees

4. They _____ on a flower.
   land lands

5. The flower _____ pink.
   is are

Grammar in Writing

When you proofread your writing, be sure you have written the correct verb to go with each pronoun.

Write to Express

✔ **Ideas** When you plan a **story**, think about your characters. How do they look? What do they like? What problem do they have?

Deval drew pictures of his characters. Then he wrote clear details about them.

Exploring a Topic

friends

fly fast

like nectar

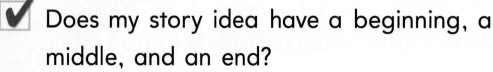

Prewriting Checklist

✔ Did I write details to describe my characters?

✔ Did I plan a problem my characters will solve?

✔ Does my story idea have a beginning, a middle, and an end?

Look for a problem Deval's characters will solve in his Story Map. Now make a Story Map for your own story. Use the Checklist.

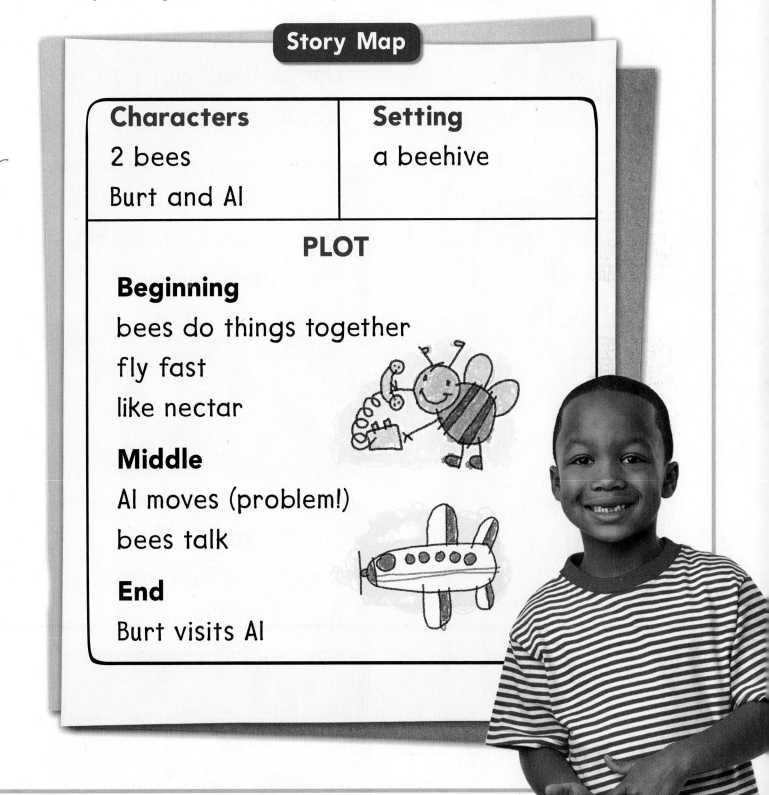

Story Map

Characters	Setting
2 bees Burt and Al	a beehive

PLOT

Beginning

bees do things together

fly fast

like nectar

Middle

Al moves (problem!)

bees talk

End

Burt visits Al

✓ **WORDS TO KNOW**

HIGH-FREQUENCY WORDS

city

myself

school

party

seven

buy

please

family

Vocabulary
Reader

Context
Cards

Words to Know

Read Together

- Read each Context Card.

- Use a blue word to tell about something you did.

1

city

They moved to the city from the country.

2

myself

I took the box into the house all by myself.

3 school
He met many new friends at school.

4 party
They had a party for their new classmate.

5 seven
She will bring seven apples to school.

6 buy
She will buy a plant for her friend.

7 please
"Please play with us," they said.

8 family
They invited the family to come in.

Background

✔ **WORDS TO KNOW** **Moving Away**

What might happen if your family moved to a new city? You might need seven boxes to pack your things. You might ask, "Can I pack these myself, please?" At your old school, friends might have a party for you and buy you a gift!

What would you pack if you were moving? What would remind you of your old friends?

Comprehension

✔ **TARGET SKILL** **Understanding Characters**

Remember that you can learn a lot about story **characters** from the things they say and do. Use what characters say and do as clues to figure out how they feel and why they act as they do.

Characters: boy, girl, king, queen
What other characters could be in this story?

As you read **The New Friend**, find out about the new friend and what the boys say, do, and feel.

Speaking	Acting	Feeling

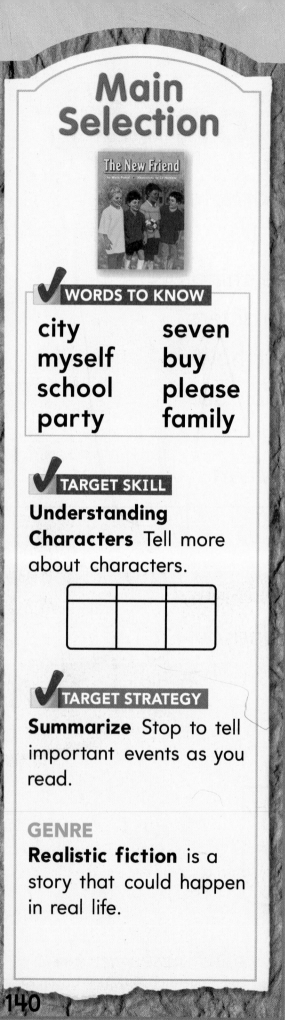

The New Friend

✔ WORDS TO KNOW

city	seven
myself	buy
school	please
party	family

✔ TARGET SKILL

Understanding Characters Tell more about characters.

✔ TARGET STRATEGY

Summarize Stop to tell important events as you read.

GENRE

Realistic fiction is a story that could happen in real life.

Meet the Author

María Puncel

María Puncel lives in Spain. She writes her books in Spanish. Many of them have been translated into English, including **El Amigo Nuevo**.

Meet the Illustrator

Ed Martinez

Ed Martinez grew up with a painter in the family. His father was an artist! As a boy, Mr. Martinez got started by drawing horses. Now he draws pictures for magazines and books.

The New Friend

by María Puncel • illustrations by Ed Martinez

Essential Question

What clues tell you what a character is like?

Martin, Luis, and I lived in the city. Next door was an old house. No one had lived there for a long time.

One day a work crew came with pails and brushes. They started to wash and paint the empty house.

After they were done, and the paint had dried, the house looked pretty and new.

The next day a big truck pulled up. It was full of crates and boxes. A crew unloaded the boxes off the truck. A new family would soon live there.

Today Luis went over to the house next door.
He met a boy called Makoto. Then we all met
Makoto. Makoto was seven years old—just
like us.

Before long, we found out that Makoto played
soccer. He could keep running and running.
He was good at learning things, too. He learned
all of our names by the end of the game.

Soon Makoto's family was all moved in. We met his mother and father. They were glad that Makoto had made some new friends.

✔️ **STOP AND THINK**

Understanding Characters
Why are Makoto's parents glad Makoto made new friends?

148

While Makoto's mother and father went to buy food, Makoto stayed and played with us.

When Makoto's mother and father rejoined us, Martin, Makoto, and I helped them carry the bags into the house.

Makoto said he would show us around his house. Then we went up to look at Makoto's room.

Makoto still had a lot of boxes to unpack. He had some nice toys and kites. He said that on the next windy day, we could bring his kites outside and fly them. He said I could fly a kite by myself.

Then we went outside to look
at Makoto's pictures from Japan.
He had them in a green book.

On the first page, we saw Makoto's old house in Japan. On the next page, we saw Makoto's family in Japan. The last page had pictures of Makoto's friends. They showed Makoto's seventh birthday party. Makoto said he wishes we could meet his old friends.

At the end of the day, Makoto's mother and
father repaid us for helping—with cookies!
We said "please" and "thank you" and ate up.

Makoto's father said he had a new job in the
city. Makoto would be going to our school.
We were all glad about that!

We said good-bye to Makoto and his mother and father. Then we went home to our families. We were glad to have a new friend next door.

What Would You Do?

New in School Makoto's new friends help make him feel welcome. How would you make a new student feel welcome at your school? Act it out with a partner. Take turns playing the new student. PARTNERS

Turn and Talk — Describe Makoto

Read pages 146–147 again with a partner. What do you learn about Makoto? Tell how the pictures and words give you clues about what he is like. Do you think Makoto will like his new home?

UNDERSTANDING CHARACTERS

Connect to Social Studies

✓ **WORDS TO KNOW**

city	seven
myself	buy
school	please
party	family

GENRE

Informational text gives facts about a topic. Find facts about neighborhoods in this magazine article.

TEXT FOCUS

A **map** is a drawing of a town, state, or other place. Find your state on the map.

Neighborhoods

by Isabel Collins

Many people live, work, and go to school in a neighborhood. American cities have many neighborhoods. Two of these cities are San Francisco and Laredo. Where does your family live?

Cherry Blossom Festival in Japantown, San Francisco

San Francisco

Japantown is a neighborhood in the city of San Francisco. Many Japanese Americans live there.

Japantown has a Cherry Blossom Festival in the spring. It is like a big party. You can buy Japanese food and enjoy Japanese music, art, and dances.

United States

San Francisco

Texas

California

Laredo

Laredo

Many Mexican Americans live in the city of Laredo. It is called the "Gateway to Mexico." Laredo has had seven flags throughout history.

Each year there is a big festival to celebrate George Washington's birthday. There are pageants, concerts, and parades like this one. I like the Jalapeño Eating Contest, myself!

Save me some jalapeños, please!

Making Connections

Read Together

Text to Self

Make a Map Make a map of your neighborhood that shows the places where you have fun.

Text to Text

Talk About Neighborhoods What are some places in a neighborhood where friends can play? Talk about this with a partner. Listen to each other.

Text to World

Connect to Social Studies What changes happen when people move to a new country? What stays the same?

Grammar

Read Together

Contractions A **contraction** is a short way of writing two words. This mark (') takes the place of missing letters.

It is a very big truck!
It's a very big truck!

He is helping his dad.
He's helping his dad.

This box is not too heavy.
This box **isn't** too heavy.

I do not know what is in it.
I **don't** know what is in it.

Write the contractions for the underlined words. Use another sheet of paper.

1. <u>I am</u> happy to meet a new friend.

2. Today <u>he is</u> moving next door.

3. Jamal <u>is not</u> finished unpacking.

4. I <u>do not</u> know what games he likes.

5. His toys <u>are not</u> on the shelves yet.

Grammar in Writing

When you proofread your writing, be sure you have written contractions correctly.

Write to Express

✔ **Sentence Fluency** A good **story** usually has some short sentences and some long ones.

Deval drafted a story about two friends. Later, he made a long sentence by joining two short sentences with **and**.

Revised Draft

Burt packed his six
,and
mittens. He got on a jet.

Revising Checklist

 Did I write some short and long sentences?

 Does my story have a beginning, a middle, and an end?

Did I write the exact words a character says?

 Did I write contractions correctly?

164

Find short and long sentences in Deval's story. Use the Checklist to revise your draft.

Final Copy

Best Friends

Burt and Al were friends. They flew fast. They liked nectar. Then things changed. Al moved to a hive up north. Burt phoned Al. "I'm so sad," he said. Soon they had an idea. Burt packed his six mittens, and he got on a jet.

Read the next two selections. Then tell what causes events to happen in each selection.

An Old Friend

Tadpole and Fish are friends. They like to swim in the pond. One day, Fish goes out to look for Tadpole. She cannot find him. She is very upset.

The weeks pass by. Fish swims all by herself. Then she hears a big PLOP! A frog swims up to her.

"Fish!" the frog says. "I was looking for you."

"Do I know you?" Fish asks.

"Yes," says the frog. "I am your old friend, Tadpole. Now I am a frog. I grew up!"

"I missed you!" says Fish. "I am glad you found me, Frog."

Greeting Butterfly Visitors

Each fall, monarch butterflies fly south to Mexico. They go there for the winter because it is warm. It can be a long trip to Mexico. The butterflies make stops in towns along the way.

Some towns have a big party to greet the butterflies! People dress up in orange and black, the colors of the monarch. People may dress as caterpillars or flowers, too. The people dance and sing together. They look for the butterflies.

People put tags on some of the butterflies when they stop by. This helps us learn more about the long trip each butterfly takes.

Unit 5 Wrap-Up

Read Together

The Big Idea

Watch How a Plant Grows! Fill a cup with dirt. Bury a bean seed in the dirt. Then water it well and put the cup in a sunny spot. Measure the plant each week. Make a graph to show the plant's growth.

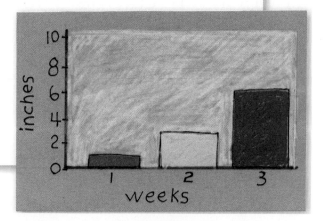

Listening and Speaking

People Change Think of all the ways you have changed since you were a baby. Use actions, sounds, and words to show a small group how you have changed.

Words to Know

Unit 5   High-Frequency Words

21 "The Tree"

told	thought
night	better
pretty	turned
window	saw

24 A Butterfly Grows

ready	places
anything	also
upon	flower
kind	warm

22 Amazing Animals

learning	young
begins	follow
until	years
eight	baby

25 The New Friend

city	seven
myself	buy
school	please
party	family

23 Whistle for Willie

house	father
along	again
together	nothing
boy	began

Glossary

A

amazing
Something **amazing** will cause surprise. It is **amazing** to see a shooting star.

awful
Awful means very bad or terrible. I had an **awful** pain in my side, so I went to the doctor.

B

beautiful
Beautiful means nice to see or hear. The garden was full of **beautiful** flowers.

brushes
A **brush** is a tool that is used for scrubbing. We use the **brushes** to scrub the floors.

E

empty

Empty means with nothing inside. When I opened the box, it was **empty**.

errand

An **errand** is a special trip you take to do something. I ran an **errand** for my mom.

G

grocery

A **grocery** store is where you buy food. Luke stopped at the **grocery** store to pick up some bread for dinner.

H

happened

To **happen** means to take place. Mr. Chow read about what **happened** in the park.

L

lemonade

Lemonade is a drink made from lemons.
I like to drink **lemonade** on a hot day.

llama

A **llama** is an animal that looks like
a camel. My aunt has a pet **llama**
on her ranch.

M

milkweed

Milkweed is a kind of plant with a white juice. Monarch
caterpillars eat **milkweed** leaves.

monarch

A **monarch** is a kind of butterfly. A **monarch** butterfly
has orange, black, and white wings.

P

pails

A **pail** is something you use to carry things. The people used **pails** to carry water to put out the fire.

pleased

Pleased means to be made happy. Ms. Perez was **pleased** when her students did so well.

pocket

A **pocket** is a small bag of cloth. I always keep my money in the **pocket** of my pants.

polar bear

A **polar bear** is a large white bear that lives where it is cold. A **polar bear** will roll in the snow to clean its fur.

porcupine

A **porcupine** is an animal that is covered with long sharp quills. Most animals will leave a **porcupine** alone.

R

rejoined

To **rejoin** means to get together again. We **rejoined** the group after we finished our chores.

repaid

To **repay** means to give something back. I **repaid** my brother for the money he loaned me.

S

seventh

If something is **seventh**, that means that there are six things before it. Saturday is the **seventh** day of the week.

shadow

A **shadow** is a dark area with light around it. The sun made a **shadow** behind the tree.

soccer

Soccer is a game where players kick a ball. Nina was a very good **soccer** player because she was fast.

staked

To **stake** means to use a pointed stick to help something stand up. Andrea **staked** the plant to help it grow straight.

stroked

To **stroke** means to rub gently. Matt **stroked** the puppy to make it calm down.

T

themselves

Themselves means those people or animals. As animals get older, they can take care of **themselves**.

toes

Toes are the parts of the foot that help people and animals walk. People have five **toes** on each foot.

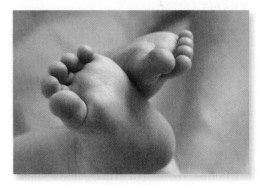

U

unloaded
To **unload** means to take off. The woman **unloaded** the bags of food from the car.

unpack
To **unpack** means to take out of a box or a suitcase. We started to **unpack** the boxes in the kitchen.

W

whirled
To **whirl** means to spin or to turn in circles. My little brother **whirled** and whirled until he was dizzy.

Acknowledgments

"Caballito blanco, reblanco/Little White Horse" from *Mamá Goose: A Latino Nursery Treasury* by Alma Flor Ada and F. Isabel Campoy. Text copyright © 2004 by Alma Flor Ada and F. Isabel Campoy. Reprinted by permission of Hyperion Books for Children. All rights reserved.

The New Friend, originally published as *El Amigo Nuevo* by Maria Puncel, illustrated by Ulises Wensell. Copyright © 1995 Laredo Publishing Company. Reprinted by permission of Laredo Publishing Company, Inc.

"Pet Snake" by Rebecca Kai Dotlich from *A Pet For Me*, published by HarperCollins. Copyright © 2003 by Rebecca Kai Dotlich. Reprinted by permission of Curtis Brown, Ltd.

"The Tree" from *Poppleton Forever* by Cynthia Rylant, illustrated by Mark Teague. Text copyright © 1998 by Cynthia Rylant. Illustrations copyright © 1998 by Mark Teague. All rights reserved. Reprinted by permission of Blue Sky Press, a division of Scholastic, Inc.

Whistle for Willie by Ezra Jack Keats. Copyright © 1964 by Ezra Jack Keats. All rights reserved including the right of reproduction in whole or in part in any form. Reprinted by permission of Viking Children's Books, a member of Penguin Young Readers Group, a division of Penguin Group (USA), Inc.

Credits

Photo Credits

Placement Key: (t) top; (b) bottom; (l) left; (r) right; (c) center; (bkgd) background; (frgd) foreground; (i) inset.

8a (c)Michael S. Quinton/Getty Images; **8b** spread (c)Scott Nielsen/Bruce Coleman USA; **8b** (c)Michael S. Quinton/Getty images; **10** (t) (c)Gary Crabbe/Alamy; **10** (b) (c)Gail Jankus/Photo Researchers, Inc.; **11** (tl) (c)imagebroker/Alamy; **11** (tr) (c)Mark Bolton/Corbis; **11** (cl) (c)John Henley/Corbis; **11** (cr) (c)Omni Photo Communications Inc./IndexStock; **11** (bl) (c) Comstock /SuperStock; **11** (br) (c)Scott Barrow/Corbis; **11** (cl inset) (c)Siede Preis/Photodisc; **12** (c) Katrina Brown/Alamy; **13** (c)Gary W. Carter/Corbis; **14** (t) (c)Courtesy of Cynthia Rylant; **14** (b) (c)Courtesy of Mark Teague; **32** (t) (c)A & M SHAH/Animals Animals - Earth Scenes; **32** (b) (c)Joe McDonald/CORBIS; **33** (tl) (c)Steve Maslowski/Visuals Unlimited/Getty Images; **33** (tr) (c)blickwinkel/Alamy; **33** (cl) (c)Beverly Joubert/National Geographic/Getty Images; **33** (cr) (c)Gavriel Jecan/ Photographer's Choice/Getty Images; **33** (bl) (c)DLILLC/Corbis; **33** (br) (c) Keren Su/China Span/Alamy; **34** (tl) Getty Images/Photodisc; (tcl) (c)Siede Preis/Photodisc; (tcr) Corbis; (tr) (c) ImageState/Alamy; (bl) Photodisc; (bcl) Digital Vision/Getty Images; (bcr) Photodisc; (br) Stockbyte/Getty Images; **35** (c) Ariel Skelley/Blend Images/Alamy; **36** (inset) (c) Hmco/John Lei; **36-37** (c)Stephen J. Kraseman/Photo Researchers, Inc; **38-39** (c)Alan Carey/Photo Researchers, Inc.; **40-41** (c)Nigel J. Dennis/Photo Researchers, Inc.; **42-43** (c)Gay Bumgarner/Tips Images; **46-47** (c)Bonnie Sue Rauch / Photo Researchers, Inc.; **48-49** (c)George & Judy Manna / Photo Researchers, Inc.; **52-53** (c)Mitch Reardon/Photo Researchers, Inc; **54** (c)Gary Randall/Taxi/Getty Images; **55** (inset) (c)Stephen J. Kraseman/Photo Researchers, Inc.; **56** (inset) (c) Ariel Skelley/Getty Images;